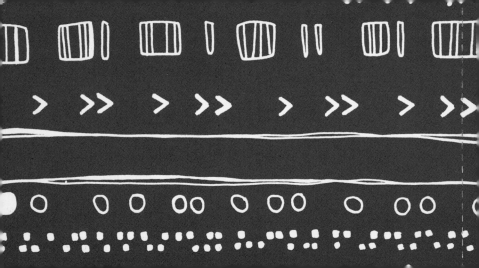

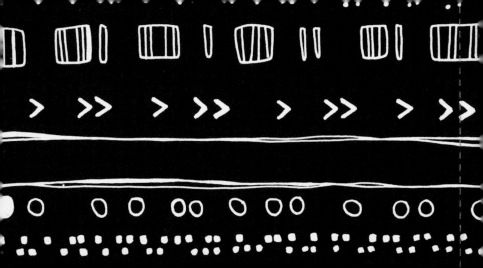

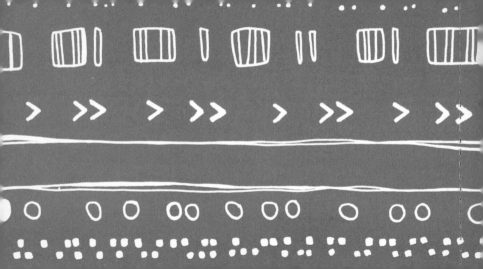

good for:

A NIGHT FREE FROM
COOKING and DISHWASHING

INSTEAD... (CHOOSE ONE):

- Step to the stove, Julia Child
- Make a reservation, you're taking me out
- I'm feeling Italian tonight. Pizza?

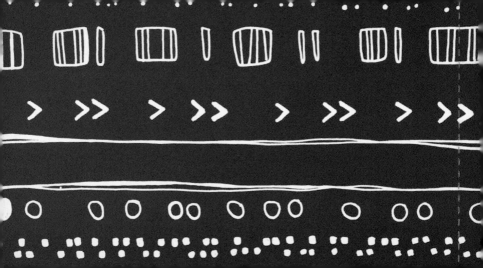

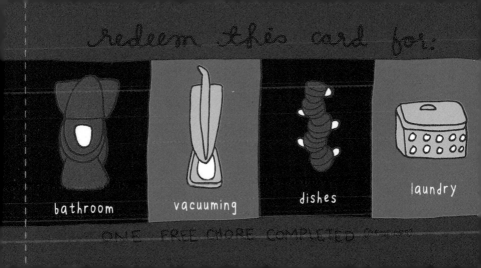

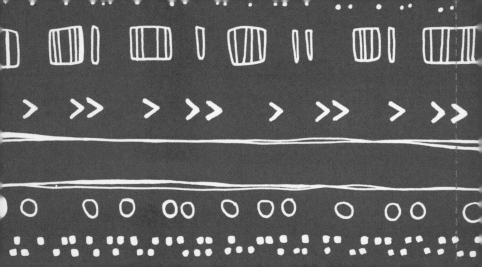

A LATE-NIGHT DRUGSTORE TRIP

EMBARRASSING ESSENTIALS MAY BE INCLUDED WITH PURCHASE

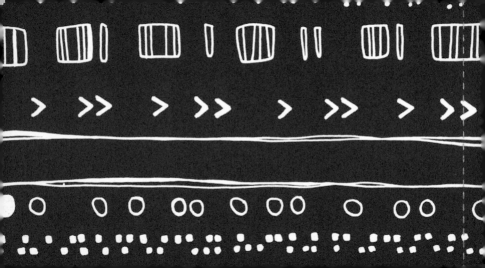

- REDEEM THIS CARD FOR -

A

HIGH - SCHOOL STYLE

make-out session

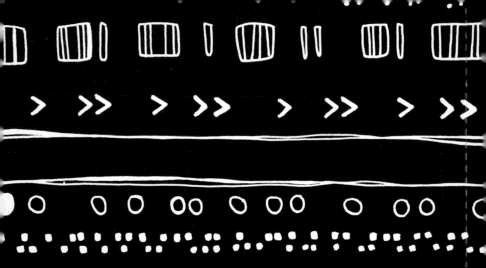

redeem this card for

—ONE EVENING—
of complete control
OF THE REMOTE ✱

✱ Exceptions for

apply in some households

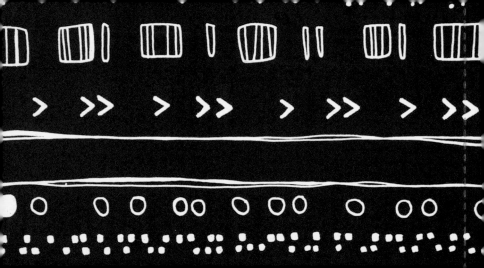

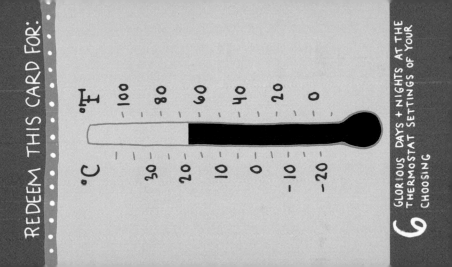

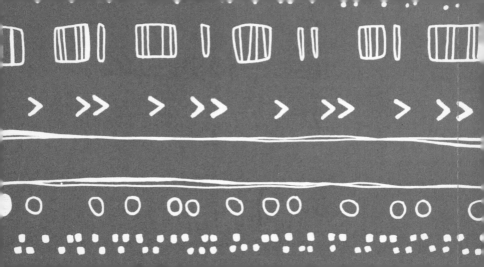

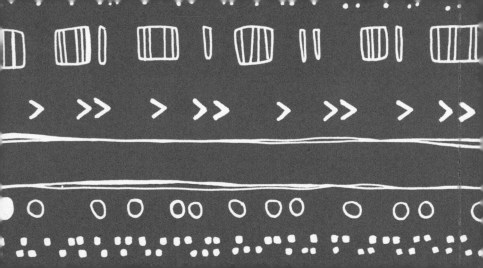

-REDEEM THIS CARD FOR-

one incredible mind-bending

DISAPPEARING ACT

(SO YOU CAN INVITE YOUR FRIENDS OVER)

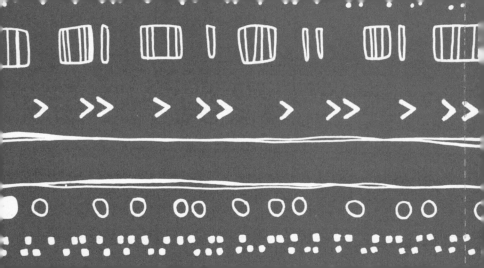

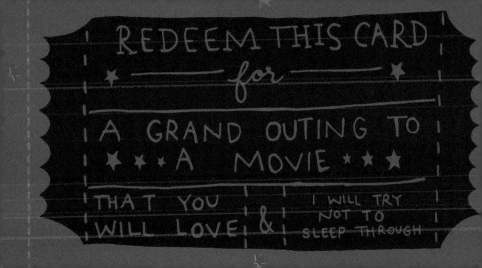

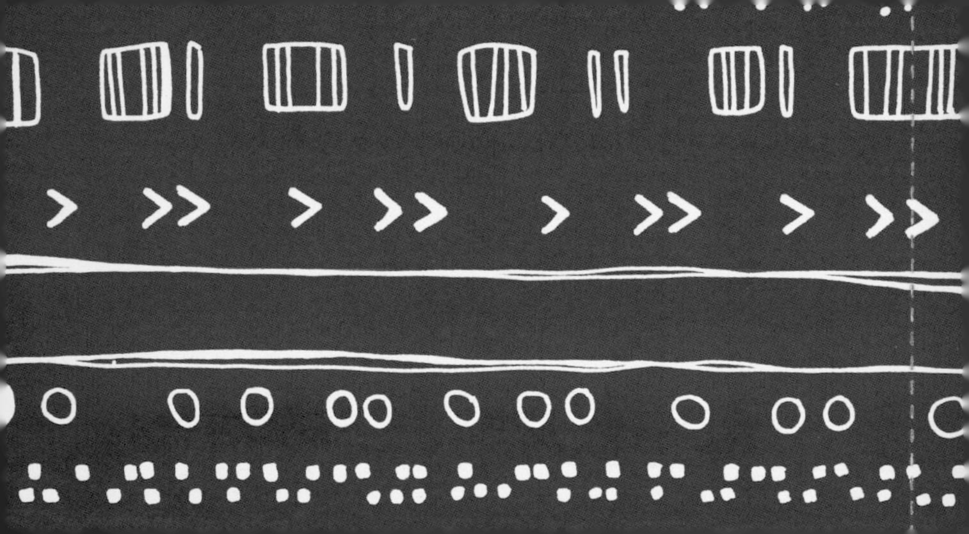

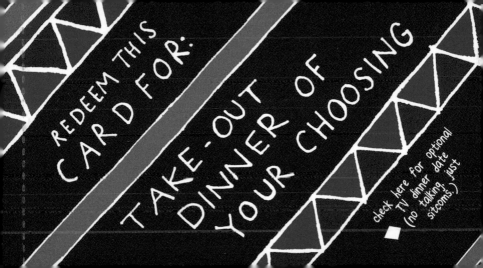

REDEEM THIS CARD FOR:

TAKE-OUT DINNER OF YOUR CHOOSING

check here for optional
TV dinner date
(no talking; just
sitcoms.)

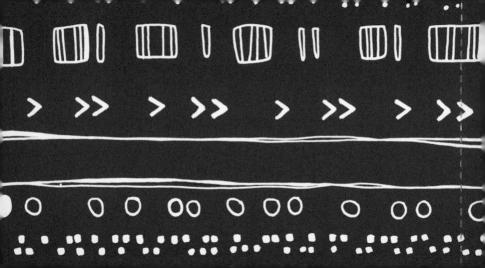

REDEEM THIS CARD FOR

ONE

RELAXINGLY

mediocre

SHOULDER RUB

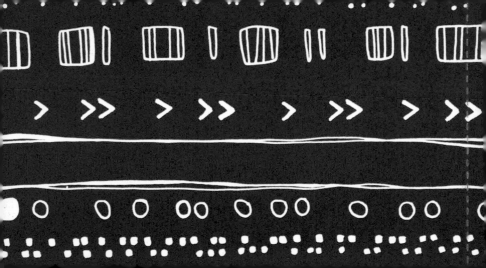

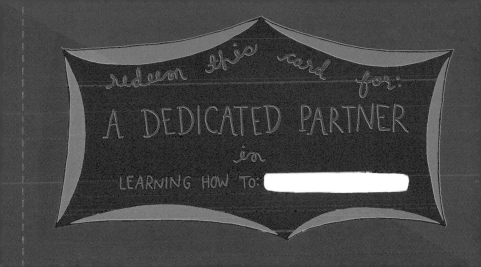

redeem this card for:

A DEDICATED PARTNER

in

LEARNING HOW TO:

GOOD FOR:

a PLAY-by-PLAY RECREATION OF
THIS *blast-from-the-past*
DATE: [   ]

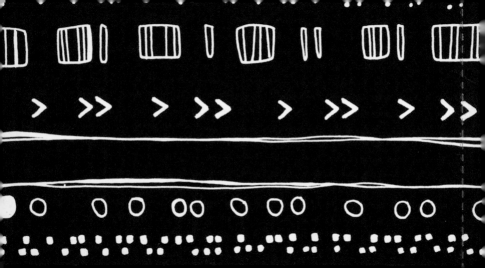

SHOW THAT SPECIAL SOMEONE HOW MUCH YOU CARE!

$7.95 US

ISBN 978-1-61243-398-1

50795

9 781612 433981

Published by Ulysses Press   Printed in China

personalized coupons to
TEAR OUT,
— CASH IN →
and make the day
a whole lot sweeter